First Ladies

Lady Bird Johnson

Jennifer Strand

Launch!
An Imprint of Abdo Zoom
abdopublishing.com

abdopublishing.com

Published by Abdo Zoom, a division of ABDO, PO Box 398166, Minneapolis, Minnesota 55439.
Copyright © 2019 by Abdo Consulting Group, Inc. International copyrights reserved in all countries.
No part of this book may be reproduced in any form without written permission from the publisher.
Launch!™ is a trademark and logo of Abdo Zoom.

Printed in the United States of America, North Mankato, Minnesota.

052018
092018

THIS BOOK CONTAINS
RECYCLED MATERIALS

Photo Credits: Alamy, AP Images, LBJ Library, ©Frank Wolfe p18

Production Contributors: Kenny Abdo, Jennie Forsberg, Grace Hansen, John Hansen

Design Contributors: Dorothy Toth, Neil Klinepier

Library of Congress Control Number: 2017961165

Publisher's Cataloging-in-Publication Data

Names: Strand, Jennifer, author.

Title: Lady Bird Johnson / by Jennifer Strand.

Description: Minneapolis, Minnesota : Abdo Zoom, 2019. | Series: First ladies |
    Includes online resources and index.

Identifiers: ISBN 9781532122842 (lib.bdg.) | ISBN 9781532123825 (ebook) |
    ISBN 9781532124310 (Read-to-me ebook)

Subjects: LCSH: Johnson, Lady Bird, 1912-2007, Biography--Juvenile literature. | Presidents' spouses--
    United States--Biography--Juvenile literature. | First ladies (United States)--Biography--Juvenile
    literature.

Classification: DDC 973.9230 [B]--dc23

Table of Contents

Lady Bird Johnson

Lady Bird Johnson was a First Lady of the United States. Her husband Lyndon B. Johnson was the 36th US president. She is known for her national **beautification** projects.

Early Life

Claudia Taylor was born on December 22, 1912. She grew up in Karnack, Texas.

A family nurse once said that Claudia was as "purty as a ladybird." The nickname stuck.

Lady Bird was well-educated. She earned two **degrees**. She was active on campus.

She met Lyndon B. Johnson
in 1934. They were married
that same year. They had
two children together.

Leader

Lady Bird helped pay for Lyndon's first election run. Lyndon was elected to **Congress** in 1937.

They moved from Texas to Washington, DC.

Lady Bird ran Lyndon's office while he served in **World War II**.

Lyndon became Vice President in 1961. Lady Bird traveled to many countries. She spoke at many events.

First Lady

Lady Bird Johnson was First Lady from 1963 to 1969. She backed many environmental causes.

She created an **act** to fix US highways in 1965. It was the first act started by a First Lady. In 1969, she became a member of the National Park Services.

Legacy

After leaving office, Lady Bird was given the Medal of Freedom. She also received the Congressional Gold Medal. These are the highest awards a person can get.

17

In 1982, she opened the National Wildflower Research Center. It was renamed the Lady Bird Johnson Wildflower Center in 1997.

Lady Bird Johnson

Born: December 22, 1912

Birthplace: Karnack, Texas

Husband: Lyndon B. Johnson

Years Served: 1963–1969

Political Party: Democratic

Known For: Johnson was a First Lady of the United States. She focused on national beautification projects and supporting women's rights.

Key  Dates

1912: Claudia Taylor is born on December 22.

1934: Lady Bird marries Lyndon B. Johnson on November 17.

1961-1963: Lady Bird Johnson is Second Lady while John F. Kennedy is president.

1963-1969: Lady Bird Johnson is the First Lady. Lyndon B. Johnson is the 36th president.

1982: Johnson opens the National Wildflower Research Center.

2007: Lady Bird Johnson dies on July 11.

Glossary

act – rules put down on paper. If passed, they are turned into law.

beautification – the act of making a place or thing look better.

Congress – the body that makes the laws for the United States. It includes the House of Representatives and the Senate.

degree – a title given by a college, university, or trade school to its students for completing their studies.

environmental – relating to the natural world and the impact of human activity on its condition.

World War II – a war fought in Europe, Asia, and Africa from 1939 to 1945.

Online Resources

For more information on
Lady Bird Johnson, please visit
abdobooklinks.com

Learn even more with the
Abdo Zoom Biographies database.
Visit **abdozoom.com** today!

Index